Dolley Madison Saves George Washington

WRITTEN AND ILLUSTRATED BY DON BROWN

Houghton Mifflin Company

Boston 2007

For Beth, Thom, Nick, Danny, and Braeden, with love.

www.houghtonmifflinbooks.com

The text of this book is set in Mrs. Eaves Roman.
The illustrations are pen and ink and watercolor on paper, as well as digitally created.
Book design by Carol Goldenberg

Library of Congress Cataloging-in-Publication Data

Brown, Don.
Dolley Madison saves George Washington / written and illustrated by Don Brown.
p. cm.
ISBN-13: 978-0-618-41199-3 (hardcover)
ISBN-10: 0-618-41199-2 (hardcover)
1. Madison, Dolley, 1768–1849—Juvenile literature. 2. Presidents' spouses—United States—
Biography—Juvenile literature. 3. Washington, George, 1732–1799—Portraits—Juvenile literature.
4. Washington (D.C.)—History—Capture by the British, 1814—Juvenile literature. I. Title.
E342.1.B76 2007
973.8'1092—dc22
[B]
2006009813
Printed in Singapore
TWP 10 9 8 7 6 5 4 3 2 1

EVERYBODY TALKED ABOUT DOLLEY MADISON.

They talked about her charm and grace.

They talked about her beauty, her stunning gowns, and her delightful banquets.

"Everybody loves Mrs. Madison. That's because Mrs. Madison loves everybody," they said.

It was a surprising turn for the onetime farm girl whose early years had not included grand parties and fancy clothes. Then she married James Madison in 1794 and joined his hectic political life.

James Madison was a great man of the Revolution, a Founding Father. In the early days of the American republic, he became President Thomas Jefferson's secretary of state. Jefferson, a widower with no wife of his own, enlisted Dolley to be something of his first lady and entertain politicians and foreign leaders.

She threw wonderful dinner parties, and even honored Lewis and Clark with a celebration before their daunting overland journey to the Pacific Ocean. Dolley became the capital's leading hostess.

Dolley's reputation grew when James Madison became president in 1808. As the *actual* first lady, she arranged weekly get-togethers; "drawing rooms," she called them.

Good-natured Dolley treated all her guests like family or long-lost friends, and she had "a smile and a pleasant word for everybody." Her beautiful gowns and outrageous turbans of satin and gold and ostrich feathers dazzled all. Everyone ached to attend the drawing rooms.

Despite the busy social whirl, Dolley still had the President's Mansion to manage. She saw a sore need for redecorating and threw herself to the task. Custom-made furniture, hand-woven carpet, and velvet curtains were carefully selected. In the dining room, she reserved a place for a remarkable lifesize portrait of George Washington.

The painting by the well-known artist Gilbert Stuart had been in the mansion since 1800. It portrayed the first president not like a king but as the country's leading private citizen, highlighting America's preference for democracy instead of royalty. The painting also showed the respect and love everyone had for Washington, feelings that Dolley surely shared. In fact, Washington was more than a war hero and great statesman to Dolley: she was related to him through her sister's marriage to Washington's nephew.

But in 1812, talk of Dolley's redecorating, her glamorous clothes, and her drawing rooms paled beside a bitter American and English quarrel. Each country felt the other meant it harm . . .

Finally the arguments exploded into war. Battles blazed on land and sea. Then, in 1814, Britain invaded America and thousands of English soldiers stalked the Washington, D.C., countryside. Dolley's terrified friends fled.

Dolley did not.

August 22 found her with spyglass in hand at the top window of the President's Mansion, "watching with unwearied anxiety" for the president, her dear husband, in the field with his army.

She later wrote that she saw only "groups of military wandering in all directions, as if there was lack of arms, or the spirit to fight!"

Suddenly a dust-covered messenger on horseback galloped up to the president's house and warned that the British were near.

The one hundred soldiers that were supposed to be guarding the presidential mansion ran off.

Dolley did not.

Deserted by nearly everyone, Dolley must have had the good sense to run away, too. And who would expect otherwise from her? She was not a soldier but a socialite, more familiar with the whistle of flutes than the whistle of bullets. But in that moment she leapt to action, grabbing important government papers and other valuables to rescue.

Then she remembered George Washington.

Dolley refused to surrender the cherished painting to the sure destruction by the English soldiers. Delaying her escape, she commanded two servants to take the portrait from the wall.

They fumbled with the screws.

Dolley ordered the frame broken.

The men shattered the wood with a hatchet and freed the painting. Two good citizens appeared, and Dolley instructed them to *"save that picture."* Only then did she race for safety.

Dashing through the city,

she met James near the banks of the Potomac River.

Before he returned to the fighting, the couple
promised to reunite later at a distant tavern.

The city of Washington burned and flames lit the distant sky.

Dolley took to the roads jammed with fleeing wagons and carts.

Dolley made her way to the tavern, but instead of James she found a crowd of outraged women who blamed the president for the fighting and destruction by the British.

"Your husband has got mine out fighting," they bawled. "You shan't stay in this house, so get out!"

Dolley retreated to another inn, arriving just as "black thunder muttered, forked lightning flashed, [and] hurricane blasts announced [a] tornado which . . . broke forth with tropical fury."

Disguised as a simple farm woman,

Dolley escaped to the countryside
as the British ransacked Washington.

She returned after several days, later saying, "I cannot tell you what I felt on re-entering [the capital]—such destruction, such confusion. The [British] fleet full in view and . . . at night the rockets were seen flying near us."

She and James reunited.

They mourned the destruction of Washington but took heart from an American victory at Baltimore Harbor in Maryland. An onlooker there, Francis Scott Key, described the battle in a poem that would eventually become the national anthem.

When people learned there was more to Dolley Madison than satin gowns and dainty cakes, they called her one of the bravest soldiers of the war.

Months later, the British and Americans ended their war. The burned President's Mansion would be rebuilt, its charred sandstone walls painted white, prompting people to call it the White House.

Dolley went on throwing more parties, and met or befriended almost every important person in America's early history, including the first eleven presidents.

James Madison

James Monroe

John Quincy Adams

Andrew Jackson

Martin Van Buren

Thomas Jefferson

William Henry Harrison

John Adams

John Tyler

George Washington

Dolley Madison 1768-1849

James Polk

And what became of the George Washington portrait?

It escaped the British and returned to the White House, where it remains on display today—just as Dolley would have wished it.

GILBERT STUART WAS BORN in Rhode Island in 1755. At the onset of the American Revolution in 1775, Stuart moved to England to further his art study. With the help of the expatriate American painter Benjamin West, Stuart exhibited at the Royal Academy in 1777. He soon had a lively following of well-born gentlemen and ladies clamoring for a portrait.

He returned to America in 1793 and painted the brightest lights of politics and commerce. John Adams, Abigail Adams, James Monroe, John Jacob Astor, and Thomas Jefferson sat for Stuart portraits. He captured George Washington's likeness with great success, and painted several portraits of him, one of which is used on the dollar bill.

He handled his finances with considerably less skill than he did his paints, and money was always a problem. After about a thousand portraits, he died penniless in 1828. A special exhibit of his work was mounted to raise money for his widow.

Portrait of
George Washington
by Gilbert Stuart

National Portrait Gallery, Smithsonian Institution
(Art Resource, NY)

Author's Note

DOLLEY PAYNE WAS BORN in North Carolina on May 20, 1768, and grew up in Virginia. The Paynes were Quakers, and it was their faith that led them to free their slaves and move to Philadelphia. Dolley was fifteen.

The move proved unfortunate. Mr. Payne had to close his unsuccessful business, a turn of events his Quaker brethren viewed as a moral failing. Bankrupt and shunned, he soon died a broken man. Dolley's mother opened a boarding house, attracting people working for the new American government, which at the time was in the Pennsylvania city.

Young Dolley married John Todd, a lawyer, and had two sons. But after just three years of marriage, a 1793 yellow fever epidemic took her husband and youngest son.

Not long afterward, the politician Aaron Burr, a boarder of Dolley's mother, introduced Dolley to James Madison, a Founding Father of the new American republic. Madison's intellect and energy had helped secure the U.S. Constitution, and he has been called its "Father." Madison was Dolley's senior by seventeen years. Still, they fell in love and married in 1794.

After Madison's presidency, many drawing room parties, and the rescue of Washington's portrait during the War of 1812, Dolley and James retired to Madison's plantation in Montpelier, Virginia. James Madison died in 1836. Shortly afterward, Dolley returned to Washington, D.C., and renewed her renown as a delightful and entertaining hostess.

In old age, Dolley found herself battling poverty when her spendthrift adult son, John, drained her meager funds from the remains of James's faltering plantation.

Dolley Madison died on July 12, 1849, at age eighty-one.

Her tombstone, as did the documents of her birth, recorded her name as Dolley, not Dolly, or Dorothy, or Dorothea.

Bibliography

Anthony, Katherine. *Dolly Madison, Her Life and Times*. Garden City, N.Y.: Doubleday & Company, 1949.

Arnett, Ethel Stephens. *Mrs. James Madison: The Incomparable Dolley*. Greensboro, N.C.: Piedmont Press, 1972.

Côte, Richard N. *Strength and Honor: The Life of Dolley Madison*. Mount Pleasant, S.C.: Corinthian Books, 2005.

Cutts, Lucia, ed. *Memoirs and Letters of Dolley Madison: Wife of James Madison, President of the United States*. New York: Houghton Mifflin, 1895.